15 MINUTES A DAY TO A
COLOSSAL VOCABULARY

BY KATHLEEN BAHR & LISA HUGHES

■SCHOLASTIC
Teaching
Resources

NEW YORK · TORONTO · LONDON · AUCKLAND · SYDNEY
MEXICO CITY · NEW DELHI · HONG KONG · BUENOS AIRES

Cover design by Norma Ortiz
Interior design by Grafica, Inc.
Interior art by Mike Moran

ISBN 0-439-20576-X

1 2 3 4 5 6 7 8 9 10   40   09 08 07 06 05 04 03

Table of Contents

ADDITIONAL VOCABULARY ACTIVITIES

Introduction

" *Several learning activities greatly enhanced Benjamin's education during the past year. My favorite was 'Wild Words.' Mrs. Hughes would introduce new words to the students along with teaching the definitions. When my son heard the word used outside of class, he was to write the word down and take it in for a small treat. My son gained an impressive new vocabulary this way. He stood a little taller each time we used a 'Wild Word,' and he was able to recognize and define it.* "

—Merlene Pagel, Parent

Sentiments like these have been expressed over and over by parents throughout the ten years we have been using Wild Words in our classrooms. Wild Words is a program we designed to enrich students' vocabularies over the course of the school year. It's easy. It's fun. And it takes just 15 minutes each day to help students build a colossal vocabulary.

We developed this vocabulary program in order to transform the "dull" subject of vocabulary into something exciting, interesting, and challenging. Instead of memorizing word lists week after week, students participate in activities involving the construction of word meaning in context. Playing Wild Word Basketball, creating and performing the Wild Word Chant, and nominating words to "banish" from the classroom are a few examples of these enjoyable, engaging activities. Students are so enthusiastic about the program that many share the daily Wild Word with family and friends and practice the Wild Word Chant at home. Wild Words is one of our students' favorite activities, as well as one of ours.

This book will provide you with everything you need to establish a complete independent vocabulary program, supplement an existing program, or reinforce content-related vocabulary instruction or language arts skills. Wild Words can be used with all student populations, including special education and gifted and talented students. In as little as 15 minutes each day, you will see tremendous growth in your students' vocabularies. If you're looking for a way to enhance your vocabulary instruction, Wild Words will provide you with a number of exciting options!

HOW TO USE THIS BOOK

Wild Words can be used as a complete independent vocabulary program or as a supplement to your existing program and your language arts instruction. In the first half of the book, you'll find activities designed to be used with Wild Words or *any* vocabulary list. For example, Watching for Wild Words encourages students to identify Wild Words (or other vocabulary words) outside of school (see p. 22). The second half of the book contains additional activities to enhance your students' study of vocabulary and related language arts skills. For example, students create Invent-a-Word dictionaries containing words that aren't in the dictionary but should be (see pp. 64–67). Games included throughout the book add to the fun!

Each activity includes a description, materials list, and step-by-step directions. You will also find reproducible activity sheets, book breaks, display ideas, tips, variations, and extensions. The Additional Resources and Activities section contains summaries and activity suggestions for more books relating to vocabulary building (see p. 71).

Getting Started With Wild Words

Setting Up the Classroom

PLANNING AND SCHEDULING

Set aside 15 minutes each day for the introduction of a Wild Word. This is a great way to begin the day or class period. On a regular basis, select Wild Word vocabulary activities (see pp. 19–43) and additional vocabulary activities (see pp. 45–71) to reinforce and extend your vocabulary instruction.

STUDENT BOOKLETS AND DISPLAY

Before beginning the program, make a Wild Word booklet for each student, and display the Wild Words so that they are visible to the entire class. (See pp. 15–18 for display ideas.)

DIRECTIONS FOR MAKING STUDENT BOOKLETS

1. Make one copy of the cover (p. 8) for each booklet. Use brightly colored paper and laminate it, if possible.

2. Determine how many internal pages you will need for each booklet, and copy the desired number of pages (p. 9).

3. Assemble the cover and pages. Add a back cover and staple. (You'll need a heavy-duty stapler if you're making books for daily use.) Write each student's name on the cover in permanent ink.

Tip!
Be sure to copy the pages front/back. This will save paper and make the books more manageable.

Tip!
If possible, make the booklets ahead of time so you can start the program on the first day of school.

WILD WORDS

Name _____

15 Minutes a Day to a Colossal Vocabulary • Scholastic Teaching Resources

Word _____

Part of Speech _____

Definition _____

_____

_____

☆ ◎ ☆ ◎ ☆ ◎ ☆ ◎ ☆ ◎ ☆ ◎ ☆ ◎ ☆ ◎ ☆ ◎ ☆ ◎ ☆

Word _____

Part of Speech _____

Definition _____

_____

_____

☆ ◎ ☆ ◎ ☆ ◎ ☆ ◎ ☆ ◎ ☆ ◎ ☆ ◎ ☆ ◎ ☆ ◎ ☆ ◎ ☆

Word _____

Part of Speech _____

Definition _____

_____

_____

☆ ◎ ☆ ◎ ☆ ◎ ☆ ◎ ☆ ◎ ☆ ◎ ☆ ◎ ☆ ◎ ☆ ◎ ☆ ◎ ☆

Word _____

Part of Speech _____

Definition _____

_____

_____

☆ ◎ ☆ ◎ ☆ ◎ ☆ ◎ ☆ ◎ ☆ ◎ ☆ ◎ ☆ ◎ ☆ ◎ ☆ ◎ ☆

Word _____

Part of Speech _____

Definition _____

_____

_____

15 Minutes a Day to a Colossal Vocabulary • Scholastic Teaching Resources

Selecting a Wild Word

The most important thing to keep in mind when selecting a Wild Word is that it must be *meaningful to your students*. For example, the Wild Word might relate to a subject your class is studying or to an upcoming sporting event. It might be a word that is amusing or a word that comes up frequently in conversation or print. As you select Wild Words, be sure to consider your students' developmental level and interests, and include different parts of speech.

Tip!
Keep a running list of Wild Word ideas so that you will always have a Wild Word ready. Be on the watch for Wild Words. You never know where you'll find a great word!

Ideas to Help You Find Wild Words

CURRENT EVENTS

Students are naturally curious about the world around them, and they enjoy participating in discussions about current events. Select words that relate to stories of interest to students. Use them as a springboard for discussion in the classroom.

Examples: incumbent, entrepreneur, mogul

CONTENT AREAS/LITERATURE

Use a Wild Word to introduce or reinforce material you're covering in class. This works especially well when presenting concepts that are challenging to master.

Examples: photosynthesis, longitude, metaphor

HOLIDAYS

Take advantage of students' excitement surrounding the holidays by selecting Wild Words that enhance their understanding of the celebrations.

Examples: blarney, commemorate, ritual

WEATHER

Tie Wild Words to news about local, national, and international weather. This is an opportunity to integrate science, geography, and map skills.

   Examples: tsunami, intermittent, sporadic

SPECIALS TEACHERS

Ask the art, music, and physical education teachers to share interesting vocabulary words they're using with students. This is a great way to demonstrate how words can be applied in different ways across a variety of disciplines.

   Examples: motif, staccato, stamina

SYNONYMS

Enhance students' awareness of the power of word choice by providing them with more precise, interesting words to use in place of familiar, overused words.

   Examples: adhere, commence, plausible

YOUR STUDENTS

Encourage students to look for words they think would make good Wild Words. Suggest places for them to look, including books, magazines, newspapers, billboards, etc. When you select a student's word, acknowledge the student to the class. Have the student explain how the word was found.

OPTIONAL: Have the student who provided the Wild Word lead the class through the daily routine.

Sample Wild Word List

A

abhor
accolade
acronym
adamant
adaptation
adhere
afterthought
alliteration
ambivalent
annual
anomaly
anonymous
antagonist
appease
aquatic
aspire
attire
authentic

B

baffled
bamboozle
bibliophile
blarney
bogus
boisterous
boycott

C

cacophony
camaraderie
cantankerous
cavalier
cease
charisma
chortle
clandestine
cliché
collaborate
colossal
commemorate
commence
contemplate
corpulent
crucial
cuisine

D

debris
decadent
dejectedly
delicacy
desolate
detest
devour
dilapidated
diligent
diurnal
docile
dubious

E

eccentric
ecstatic
embellish
entrepreneur
epidemic
eponym
exorbitant
exotic
exquisite
extravagant

F

famished
fatal
fiasco
filigree
fissure
flabbergasted
flamboyant
fluctuate
foliage
forbid
formidable
fracas
fragment
frenzy
frugal

G

gargantuan
gawk
giddy
glutton
gratitude
guffaw
gullible

H

haphazardly
havoc
hermit
homonym
hooligan
hostile
hypothesis

I

ideal
illiterate
immaculate
immigrant
inanimate
inclement
incognito
incumbent
indelible
inevitable
ingenuity
inquire
intangible
intermittent
intrinsic
inundated
invincible
iridescent
irksome

K

kin

L

leisure
lethargic
livid
loathe
local
longitude
ludicrous
luxurious

M

malfunction
mandatory
mediocre
medley
melancholy
metamorphosis
metaphor
meticulous
milestone
minuscule
miscellaneous
mnemonic
mogul
moniker
monotonous
mortified
motif

N

nebulous
nefarious
newfangled
nonchalant
notorious
nuance

O

oasis
oblivious
obsolete
onomatopoeia
optimistic
ostentatious
ostracize
oxymoron

P

palindrome
pariah
peevishly
penultimate
perceive
perennial
perfunctorily
perjure
persnickety
photosynthesis
pilfer
plausible
plethora
poised
portmanteau
precipitation
preposterous
procrastinate
prohibit
protagonist
protrude
punctual

Q

quaint
quandary
quibble

R

ravenous
recluse
reek
relentless
reluctantly
reminisce
remorse
resolution
resume
ritual
rookie

S

sarcastically
savvy
scrutinize
serendipity
shard
sinister
skeptical
solitude
splurge
spontaneous
sporadically
staccato
stamina
subtle
succinct
succulent
surreptitiously

synchronize
synonym

T

tantalizing
tedious
tepid
tome
torment
translucent
treacherous
trivial
tsunami
turbulent

U

unanimous

V

vacillate
versatile
virulent
visible

W

warily
wistfully

Z

zany
zealous

Introducing a Wild Word

In this whole-group activity, the teacher selects and teaches a Wild Word (a meaningful, interesting word) to students each day.

MATERIALS

• Wild Word books for each student (See p. 7 for directions.)

OPTIONAL: Wild Words displayed in order (See pp. 15–17 for display ideas.)

Tip!
The basic steps for introducing a Wild Word can be followed exactly or modified to meet students' needs.

STEPS

DO AHEAD: Select the Wild Word for the day. (See pp. 10–11 for ideas to help you find Wild Words and pp. 12–13 for a sample list.) Write the Wild Word on the board at the beginning of the day or class period.

1. Have students copy the Wild Word in their Wild Word books.

2. Have students pronounce the Wild Word aloud together.

3. Ask students to guess the definition of the Wild Word. Use the Wild Word in context to help them with their guesses.

4. Record the part of speech and the definition on the board. (You may wish to have more advanced students identify the part of speech.) Use a simple, clear definition. Discuss the definition, and provide several examples of the Wild Word used in context.

5. Have students copy the part of speech and the definition in their Wild Word books. Then have students create an illustration to show the meaning of the Wild Word.

6. Call on several students to describe their illustrations.

7. Use the Wild Word throughout the day, and encourage students to do the same.

   OPTIONAL: Have students wave wildly whenever they hear or read the current Wild Word or any Wild Word presented previously.

Tip!
Be sure to discuss appropriate behavior for this activity. For example, students should not wave when a guest is speaking to the class.

VARIATION: Instead of having a daily Wild Word, implement the program on a weekly basis. You may wish to use the Wild Word program during a unit of study or other set time period.

Wild Word Displays

Before beginning the Wild Word program, designate a bulletin board or a wall to display the Wild Words for the entire year. They must be visible to your students. Every time you introduce a Wild Word, add it to your display. (Do not post Wild Words in advance.) Write the Wild Word directly on the display, or record it on a note card or sentence strip attached to the display.

The following are examples of displays we have used in our classrooms:

WILD WORDS

DIRECTIONS: Cover a bulletin board with orange paper. Make a monkey out of brown paper using the template on p. 18. (You can enlarge it with an opaque projector.) Attach the monkey to the side of the bulletin board. Make bananas out of yellow paper using the template on p. 18. Staple the bananas vertically to the bulletin board, grouping them in clusters. Each banana will hold five Wild Words written on small cards. Calculate the number of bananas you will need for the entire year. As a finishing touch, add other tropical animals and plants to the display.

Tip!
Prepare note cards or sentence strips in advance.

THE TALK OF THE TOWN

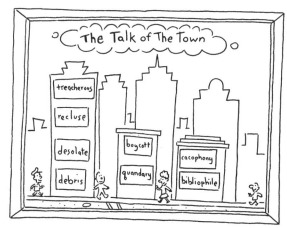

DIRECTIONS: Cover a bulletin board with blue paper. Have students design buildings (big enough to display the words), roads, cars, and people to make a city scene. Calculate how many words each building will hold, and add enough buildings to accommodate your Wild Words for the entire year.

BUILDING A STRONG VOCABULARY

DIRECTIONS: Cover a bulletin board with blue paper. Staple 12 (12" x 18") rectangles of red construction paper in rows, off-setting them to look like bricks. Each brick will hold approximately 15 Wild Words written on small cards (1.5" x 5"). Calculate the number of bricks you will need for the entire year, and display them on the bulletin board. As a finishing touch, add a bricklayer to the display.

WILD WORD JAR

DIRECTIONS: Collect Wild Words in a special Wild Word jar. Every time you introduce a Wild Word, write it on a small note card or piece of paper and put it in the jar. Use this collection of words for a variety of activities, including Wild Word Charades (p. 28), Draw a Wild Word Game (p. 29), Wild Word Part-of-Speech Sort (p. 33), and Wild Word Silly Sentences (p. 38).

Tip! ....
A large plastic ice tea container works well.

WATCHING FOR WILD WORDS

DIRECTIONS: Cover a bulletin board with blue paper. Display a "wordwatcher" looking through binoculars. Divide the bulletin board into sections. Label each section with a source students might use to find Wild Words ("Books," "Newspapers," "Magazines," "Billboards," "Television," "Internet," etc.). As students find Wild Words outside of school, list them in the appropriate sections.

Tip! ....
Include students' names with the Wild Words they find.

WORD WALL

DIRECTIONS: Cover a large section of a wall or a bulletin board with butcher paper, and divide it into eight or ten sections. Label each section with "The _____ Word," filling in the blank with your choice of categories (see below). Have students record their ideas on the display.

Examples: The Scariest Word, The Funniest Word, The Weirdest Word, The Saddest Word, The Most Beautiful Word, The Ugliest Word, The Most Overused Word, The Hardest Word to Pronounce

The Hardest Word to Pronounce -∼- surreptitiously portmanteau	The Scariest Word -∼-	The Funniest Word -∼-	The Weirdest Word -∼- persnickety	The Saddest Word -∼-	The most Beautiful word -∼-	The Ugliest word -∼-	The most overused word -∼-

Wild Word Bulletin Board Templates

Wild Word Activities

Wild Word Chant

In this whole-group activity, students create and perform a chant to help them remember Wild Words.

MATERIALS

• Wild Words posted in order (See display ideas on pp. 15–17)
• **OPTIONAL:** Wild Word book for each student

STEPS

DO AHEAD: Post the daily Wild Word in the classroom. Practice the chant using the examples below so you are familiar with the procedure.

1. After introducing the daily Wild Word (see p. 14), tell students that they are going to create and perform a group chant to help them remember the word.

2. Teach students the basic chant. Students pat their laps twice, clap twice, snap fingers twice on one hand, and snap fingers twice on the other hand for a total of eight beats. Practice the basic motion several times.

3. Explain that the chant must include the Wild Word, its definition, and an example, related comment, or humorous connection. The words will accompany the hand motions. Share several examples.

Example:

pat, pat	famished
clap, clap	very hungry
snap, snap	I think I'll raid
snap, snap	the cookie jar!

Example:

pat, pat	reek
clap, clap	smells bad
snap, snap	Dad, your feet
snap, snap	are stinky!

Example:

pat, pat	magma
clap, clap	molten lava
snap, snap	extremely
snap, snap	hot

Example:

pat, pat	flabbergasted
clap, clap	shocked and stunned
snap, snap	Oh, my goodness
snap, snap	gracious!

4. Call on three students to suggest chant ideas for the daily Wild Word.

5. Take a class vote to select the chant for the day.

6. Have students practice the day's chant several times.

7. Review past Wild Words by performing the chants for all of the Wild Words listed. As the list of Wild Words gets longer, you may start the chant from a recent Wild Word or choose a beginning and ending point.

Tip! ....

Have students vote with their heads down to encourage objectivity.

BOOK BREAK ....

Double Trouble in Walla Walla by Andrew Clements (The Millbrook Press, 1997)

When Lulu of Walla Walla opens a word warp, her English teacher doesn't know what to do. The school nurse comes to the rescue, suggesting that they say all of the "rootin'-tootin', crink'em-crank-'em, woolly-bully words" they can think of. As they try to close the word warp, the language fun begins!

EXTENSION: Share this colorful picture book with students, and have them work in pairs to create their own word warp chants using the book for ideas. Have the pairs perform their chants in front of the class.

Watching for Wild Words

In this optional homework activity, students find Wild Words outside of school and complete Wordwatching Forms. (See the Watching for Wild Words display idea on p. 17.)

OPTIONAL: Have a contest to see who can find the most Wild Words each month.

MATERIALS

- Wild Word book for each student
- One copy of the Wordwatching Form on p. 23 for each student
- Additional copies of the Wordwatching Form for later use
- Resource containing a Wild Word
- Stickers
- **OPTIONAL:** Prizes for the monthly contest

STEPS

DO AHEAD: Find an outside resource (book, magazine, newspaper, etc.) that contains a Wild Word. Make an overhead of the Wordwatching Form on p. 23.

1. Show students the resource containing a Wild Word. Read the word, tell when and where you found it, and discuss how it was used. Lead a discussion about where Wild Words can be found. Have students brainstorm ideas and list them on the board.

Examples: books, newspapers, magazines, billboards, television, radio, movies, conversations, the Internet, music, games, comic books

2. Explain to students that they are going to be "wordwatchers."

3. Distribute copies of the Wordwatching Form on p. 23. Work together to complete a Wordwatching Form using the example you provided.

> **Tip!**
> Designate a box or basket for the completed forms.

4. Show students where to find blank Wordwatching Forms, and explain how to submit the forms.

5. When a student completes a Wordwatching Form, give the student a sticker.

OPTIONAL: Tell students that the class will be holding a monthly contest to see who can find the most Wild Words outside of school. At the end of each month, award a small prize to the student who found the most Wild Words.

☆ Wordwatching Form ☆

Name _____

Word _____

Date of sighting _____

Location _____

Description of how the word was used
_____

_____

_____

_____

_____

☆ Wordwatching Form ☆

Name _____

Word _____

Date of sighting _____

Location _____

Description of how the word was used
_____

_____

_____

_____

_____

15 Minutes a Day to a Colossal Vocabulary • Scholastic Teaching Resources

Wild Word Connections

In this independent or partner activity, students think of ways Wild Words are connected and complete the Wild Word Connections worksheet.

MATERIALS

• Wild Word book containing at least 40 words for each student or pair of students
• One copy of the Wild Word Connections worksheet on p. 25 for each student or pair of students

STEPS

1. Draw three connected boxes from the Wild Word Connections worksheet on the chalkboard, and write a Wild Word in the first box. Ask students to review the definition of the word, and then encourage them to find another Wild Word that could be connected to it in some way. Call on students to share their connections and explain their ideas.

2. Select one of the suggested Wild Words, and write it in the second box. Ask students to review the connection between the two words, and write it on the line connecting the two boxes. Repeat the process for the third box.

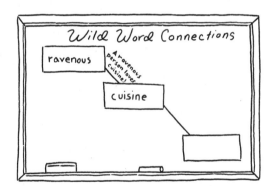 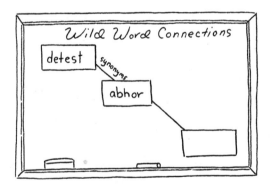

3. Distribute one copy of p. 25 to each student or pair of students. Provide students with a word to start the activity, or allow them to select one themselves.

VARIATION: WILD WORD CHAINS

Have students work independently or in pairs to make Wild Word paper chains that can be displayed in the classroom. Use two different colors of construction paper, one for the words and another for the connections. Encourage students to figure out a way to attach all of the class chains to form one giant word chain.

Tip!

In order to encourage higher-level thinking, make a list of "illegal connections," such as words starting with the same letter and words having the same number of letters.

Wild Word Connections

DIRECTIONS

Write a Wild Word in the top box. Find another Wild Word that is connected to the first word in some way, and write it in the connecting box. On the line between the two boxes, explain how the words are connected. Select another Wild Word that connects with the word in the second box, and explain how the second and third words are connected. Continue until you reach the bottom box.

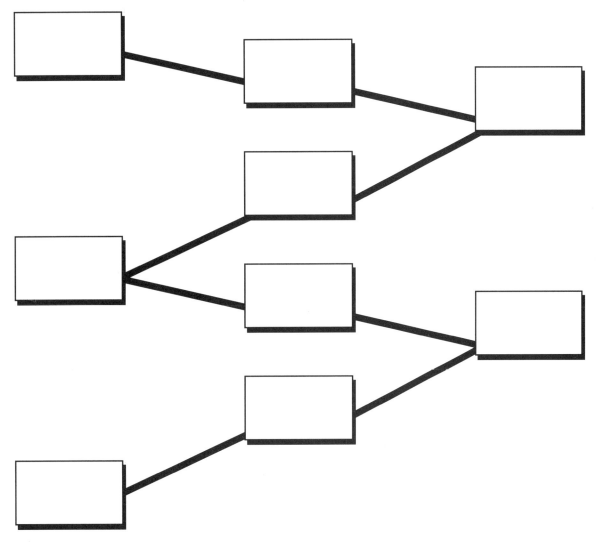

CHALLENGE

Is there a way to connect the first box with the last box? Write the connection on the back.

Wild Word Basketball

In this whole-group game, two teams of students race against each other to write a Wild Word after hearing its definition read aloud.

MATERIALS

- Wild Word book containing at least 25 words for teacher reference
- Overhead or copies of Wild Word Basketball Directions and Rules on p. 27
- Overhead projector
- Individual chalkboards or notebook paper for each student
- Basket, trash can, or large container
- Ball
- Masking tape

> **Tip!**
> A ball made of newspaper and covered with masking tape works well.

STEPS

DO AHEAD: Designate areas on the chalkboard for writing answers and keeping score. Put the basket against a wall or closed door. Mark a line with masking tape approximately ten feet away from the basket.

1. Review game directions and rules with students using p. 27.

2. Divide the class into two teams.

3. Call a student from each team to the board. Using a Wild Word book, select a Wild Word, and read its definition aloud. Have both students race to write the Wild Word that matches the definition. At the same time, have the rest of the class write the answer on individual chalkboards or notebook paper.

> **Tip!**
> To help with classroom management, teach students to cheer silently when a player on their team does well. Explain that cheering against the opposing team is forbidden and that a violation of the rules will result in a team warning. Each team will be given one warning before losing a point.

4. Call on a student in the audience to provide the correct answer. Award one point for each student at the board who gets the correct answer. (Do not award points based on spelling. This is a vocabulary game, not a spelling game.) Give the student who answered correctly first a chance to throw the ball into the basket. If the student makes the basket, his or her team earns an additional point.

5. Continue play until all students have a chance at the board. At the end of the game, announce the winning team.

VARIATION: Play this game to review spelling words. In this game, spelling counts!

Wild Word Basketball
Directions and Rules

1. The teacher calls one student at a time from each team to come to the board. Students at their desks work on individual chalkboards or on notebook paper.

2. Students listen to the teacher read the definition of a Wild Word, and then they write the word that matches the definition.

3. When students at the board finish writing their answers, they cover them with one hand and raise the other hand to show that they are finished.

4. When both students at the board have completed their answers, the teacher directs them to uncover their words. A point is awarded to each student who answered correctly. (Spelling does not count in this game.) Students then erase their work.

5. If both students at the board are correct, the one who answered first is given a chance to earn an extra point by throwing the ball into the basket. The student stands behind the designated line to shoot.

6. Play continues until all students have a chance at the board or the class period ends.

7. The team with the highest score wins the game.

Wild Word Charades

In this whole-group game, students act out Wild Words while classmates guess the words.

MATERIALS

• Wild Word book containing at least 40 words for teacher reference
• Slips of paper with selected Wild Words written on them (one for each student)
• Hat or container

STEPS

DO AHEAD: Select Wild Words that can be acted out. Write the words on slips of paper, and put them in the hat.

1. Explain that a student will draw a word from the hat and act out its meaning using gestures and movements only. After the student acts out the word, he or she will call on a classmate to guess the word and give its definition. The student who guesses the word correctly and states its meaning gets to act out the next word.

VARIATION: Instead of writing the words on slips of paper, have students select words themselves using their Wild Word books.

Tip!

Play the game in several short sessions so that every student gets a chance to participate. If a student answers correctly and has already acted out a word, have him or her select a classmate who hasn't participated.

Ludicrous!

Draw a Wild Word Game

In this whole-group game, two teams of students take turns drawing and guessing Wild Words.

MATERIALS

- Wild Word book containing at least 40 words for teacher reference
- Slips of paper with selected Wild Words written on them (one for each student)
- Container
- Clock or watch with a second hand

STEPS

DO AHEAD: Select and copy Wild Words onto slips of paper. Designate areas on the chalkboard for drawing and keeping score.

Select words you think will be the easiest and most fun to draw.

1. Divide the class into two teams.

2. Explain the rules of the game. A student from one team picks a word from the container. The student has 20 seconds to draw the word. After 20 seconds, the student's team collaborates on a guess. If the guess is correct, the student's team receives one point. If the guess is incorrect, the opposing team has a chance to guess the word. If their guess is correct, they receive the point. Play continues until the words are used *or* both teams have had an equal number of chances to draw.

3. At the end of the game, announce the winning team.

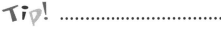

You may need to stop the game before all students have a chance to draw a word. Keep track of the score and which students went up to the board, and give the rest of the class an opportunity at a later time.

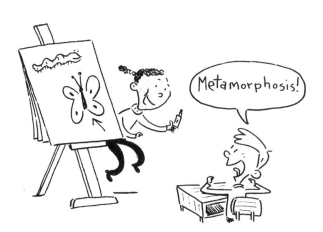

Metamorphosis!

Wild Word Bingo

In this whole-group game, students use Wild Words to play bingo.

MATERIALS

- Wild Word book containing at least 40 words for each student
- Wild Word book containing at least 40 words for teacher reference
- One copy of the bingo card on p. 31 for each student
- Markers for each student (You may wish to have students cut small squares of paper as markers.)

WILD WORD BINGO				
zany	unanimous	tepid	cease	crucial
gawk	havoc	frugal	frenzy	minuscule
local	cavalier	**free**	mediocre	precipitation
serendipity	notorious	obsolete	oxymoron	acronym
boycott	eccentric	kin	attire	gratitude

STEPS

1. Distribute copies of p. 31 and markers to each student.

2. Have students use their Wild Word books to copy one Wild Word into each box on their bingo cards. Have them copy the words in random order. When students finish filling out their bingo cards, have them put away their Wild Word books.

3. Review the rules of bingo. Explain that in order to win, a student must fill in one row across, down, or diagonally and call out "Bingo!" In addition, the winner must be able to pronounce and define each word in the winning row.

4. Begin the game by reading aloud the definition of a Wild Word. Tell students to place a marker on the word that matches the definition. As you read aloud each definition, record the corresponding word on a separate sheet of paper so that you will be able to check students' answers later.

5. Continue play until a student calls "Bingo."

6. Have the student read aloud the row of words. Use your list to verify that the words were called. (Be sure that the other students keep their markers in place in case a mistake was made.) Once the words are verified, ask the student to pronounce each word correctly and provide its definition. If the student is successful, declare him or her the winner of the game.

Tip!

Have students trade cards and play the game again. Collect and save the cards for later use.

EXTENSION: For more of a challenge, require students to cover the entire card in order to win the game.

WILD WORD BINGO

		free		

Wild Word Twenty Questions

In this whole-group game, the teacher secretly selects a Wild Word, and students try to guess the word by asking *yes* or *no* questions. The object of the game is to guess the word in 20 questions or fewer.

MATERIALS

- Wild Word book containing at least 40 words for teacher reference
- Wild Word book containing at least 40 words for each student
- Chart paper
- Markers

STEPS

1. Secretly select a Wild Word.

2. Designate a student to keep track of the number of questions asked and record the information on the chalkboard.

3. Call on students one at a time to ask *yes* or *no* questions about the selected Wild Word. The game is over when the Wild Word has been guessed or the 20-question limit has been reached. Save the score.

Examples:

Is the word related to science?
Is the word a synonym for another word?
Does the word name an action?
Does the word have three syllables?

4. Help students analyze the kinds of questions they asked. For example, ask which questions helped to narrow down the possibilities. Make a list of their ideas on chart paper.

5. Have students play the game again using their list of questions as a reference.

6. Compare scores from the two games, and discuss if it is better to guess randomly or to have a strategy in place.

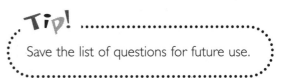

Tip! . . . .
Save the list of questions for future use.

Wild Word Part-of-Speech Sort

In this independent, partner, or whole-group activity, students classify 15–20 Wild Words according to part of speech.

MATERIALS

• Wild Word book containing at least 30 words for teacher reference
• Sentence strips or large note cards

STEPS

DO AHEAD: Write 15–20 Wild Words on sentence strips or large note cards. Be sure to include a combination of nouns, verbs, adjectives, and adverbs.

1. Post three of the words on the chalkboard. Have students read them and help you sort them according to their part of speech.

2. Have students work independently, in pairs, or as a group to classify the rest of the words according to their part of speech.

3. As a group, review the answers.

Tip!

Have students divide a piece of notebook paper into sections for each part of speech and list the Wild Words in the appropriate sections.

Wild Word Challenge Game

In this whole-group game, teams of students compete to answer questions based on Wild Words.

MATERIALS

- Wild Word book containing at least 40 words for teacher reference
- Posterboard, envelopes or construction paper, note cards, and glue to make game board
- 20 questions based on Wild Words, divided into four categories of your choice
  Examples: The Class Field Trip, Math Mania, Books We Love, Extraordinary Earth, Colorful Classmates
- Four removable cards labeled with the designated category titles
- Overhead or copies of Wild Word Challenge Game Rules and Directions on p. 35
- Overhead projector

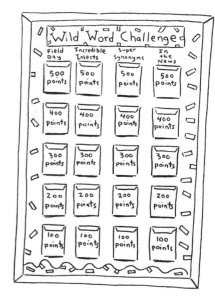

STEPS

DO AHEAD: Make a game board by attaching 20 pockets (made from envelopes or construction paper) to a large piece of posterboard. Label the pockets with five different point values (100, 200, 300, 400, 500) as shown in the example. Above each column, add a removable card labeled with one of the four designated category titles. On note cards, write five questions for each category. Organize the questions from easiest to hardest, and insert them into the pockets, starting with the 100-point pockets and ending with the 500-point pockets.

1. Divide students into teams of four to six. Have each team select a name and a spokesperson. Have each spokesperson introduce his or her team to the class. As the teams are introduced, record the team names on the board.

2. Review game directions and rules using p. 35.

3. Call on a team to start the game. Continue play until all questions have been answered or the class period is over. Record team scores on the board. At the end of the game, announce the winning team.

> **Tip!**
> Wild Words can be included in the questions. Wild Words can also be the answer to the questions. It's fun to ask questions that include school-related people and events.

Wild Word Challenge Game
Directions and Rules

DIRECTIONS

1. The teacher calls on a team to begin. To select a question, the team's spokesperson names a category and corresponding point value. The teacher reads the question and the team is given 30 seconds to discuss the answer.

2. The team's spokesperson stands up to report the answer. If the answer is correct, the team's scorekeeper records the score on the board. If the answer is incorrect, the next team is given the chance to answer the question. Another 30 seconds is provided to that team.

3. Play continues until the correct answer is provided or all teams have had the opportunity to answer the question.

4. The game ends when all questions have been answered or the class period is over. The team with the highest score wins the game.

RULES

1. The spokesperson is the only person allowed to speak for the team. If another team member calls out an answer, the team will forfeit the question.

2. Team members must whisper as they discuss answers to prevent other teams from overhearing their ideas.

Wild Word Riddles

In this independent activity, students write ten riddles using Wild Words and make a flip card to share their riddles with classmates.

MATERIALS

- Wild Word book containing at least 40 words for each student
- One copy of the Wild Word Readers worksheet on p. 37 for each student
- Scissors

STEPS

DO AHEAD: Make a list of riddle starters, and post it on the board.

Examples:

> What do you call _____?
> I name something that _____.
> I am a synonym/antonym for _____.
> What do you get when _____?

1. Explain to students that they will write ten riddles using Wild Words and make a flip card to share their riddles with classmates.

2. Ask students to share a few riddles with the class, and discuss the format in which they were written. Review the list of riddle starters, and add any new ideas.

> **Tip!**
> Check out a few riddle books from the school library, and share some riddles with the class.

3. Choose a Wild Word, and ask students to think of a riddle that has that Wild Word as the answer.

4. Distribute copies of p. 37. Have students fold the worksheet lengthwise, pressing firmly along the solid middle line so that the shorter horizontal lines are on top (like the cover of a book). With the crease on the left side, have students cut the shorter horizontal lines to make the flaps for their riddles. Explain that they will write a riddle on each top flap and the answer to the riddle on the inside under the flap.

5. Once students have completed their flip cards, have them share their Wild Word riddles with classmates.

> **Tip!**
> Display the Wild Word Riddle cards on a bulletin board or in the hallway for other students to enjoy.

Name _____

✳ ⭐ Wild Word Riddles ⭐ ✳ ☆

(1)

(2)

(3)

(4)

(5)

(6)

(7)

(8)

(9)

(10)

Wild Word Silly Sentences

In this independent or partner activity, students write and illustrate silly sentences using Wild Words.

MATERIALS

• Wild Word book containing at least 40 words for teacher reference
• Sentence strips or large note cards
• Large container
• **OPTIONAL:** Crayons or markers

STEPS

DO AHEAD: Write 25 Wild Words on sentence strips or large note cards. Be sure to include a combination of nouns, verbs, adjectives, and adverbs. Put the words in a container.

Tip!

If you're keeping words in a Wild Word jar, you can use those.

1. Have a student draw two to three words from the container and post them on the board. As a group, write a silly sentence using the words.

Examples:

If a **gargantuan** monster walked into our classroom, it's **inevitable** that students would **gawk**.

Elizabeth was **mortified** when her **boisterous** little sister **chortled** loudly in the middle of the band concert.

2. Have another student draw two to three more words from the container and post them on the board. Have students work independently or in pairs to write silly sentences using the words.

3. Call on students to share their silly sentences with the class. Repeat as desired.

OPTIONAL: Have students illustrate their silly sentences. Display student work on a bulletin board or bind it into a class book.

If a gargantuan monster walked into our classroom, it's inevitable that students would gawk.

Top Ten Wild Words

In this culminating activity, students create their own Top Ten Wild Words lists by recording their ten favorite Wild Words and the reason for each selection.

MATERIALS

• Wild Word book for each student
• Copy of a top ten list students would find interesting
• One copy of the Top Ten Wild Words worksheet on p. 40 for each student

STEPS

DO AHEAD: Find a top ten list students would find interesting.

1. Ask students to explain what a top ten list is, and have them share the types of top ten lists they've seen. Record their ideas on the board.

2. Share the top ten list you found.
OPTIONAL: Make an overhead of the list and display it.

3. Ask students to think of their favorite Wild Word. Call on a few students to share their word and tell why it's their favorite.

4. Distribute copies of p. 40. Have students complete the worksheet.

5. Have students share their Top Ten Wild Words lists with a partner or with the class.
OPTIONAL: Display the lists on a bulletin board.

EXTENSION: Compile a Top Ten Wild Words class list based on the results of this activity, and post it in the classroom.

> **Tip!**
> A top ten list can be found in newspapers such as USA Today, magazines, or on the Internet.

> **Tip!**
> Save the list to display at the class Wild Word party.

_____'s Top Ten Wild Words

1. Wild Word _____

Why I chose this word _____

_____

2. Wild Word _____

Why I chose this word _____

_____

3. Wild Word _____

Why I chose this word _____

_____

4. Wild Word _____

Why I chose this word _____

_____

5. Wild Word _____

Why I chose this word _____

_____

6. Wild Word _____

Why I chose this word _____

_____

7. Wild Word _____

Why I chose this word _____

_____

8. Wild Word _____

Why I chose this word _____

_____

9. Wild Word _____

Why I chose this word _____

_____

10. Wild Word _____

Why I chose this word _____

_____

15 Minutes a Day to a Colossal Vocabulary • Scholastic Teaching Resources

Wild Word Party

In this whole-group activity, students celebrate the year's exploration of Wild Words by hosting a party.

NOTE:
This has always been one of the *most* successful activities in our classrooms!

MATERIALS

* Wild Word book for each student
* Supplies for the invitations, decorations and activities
* **OPTIONAL:** Refreshments (including plates, cups, napkins, and utensils)

STEPS

1. Several weeks before the party, help students plan for the event. Have students design invitations and invite parents or another class to the party.

> ☆ You are invited to a ☆
> # Wild Word Party!
> **Friday, May 16, 2:00 p.m.**
> **Room 211 • Susan B. Anthony School**

Have students decide if they would like to serve refreshments. If so, designate who will bring each item, including plates, cups, napkins, and utensils.

2. A week before the party, have students plan activities for their guests. For example, they might choose to play the Wild Word Challenge Game against the guests, perform the Wild Word Chant, and share their Top Ten Wild Words lists. Have students plan and make Wild Word-related decorations.

3. On the day of the party, have students decorate the classroom, organize seating for the guests, and arrange the refreshments (if you are serving them).

4. During the party, have students and guests participate in the planned activities. Your students will be proud of the words they learned throughout the year, and your guests will be astonished by your students' extensive vocabularies!

Tip!
If you have limited space, establish the number of guests a student may invite.

Tip!
Send home a note confirming what each student will bring to the party.

Tip!
Be sure to prepare materials, such as game questions for the Wild Word Challenge Game, ahead of time.

Tip!
If you're serving refreshments, have students design a butcher paper tablecloth covered with Wild Words and illustrations for the refreshments table.

Wild Words Certificate

Award students with a Wild Words certificate at the end of the year.

MATERIALS

• One copy of the Wild Words certificate on p. 43 for each student

STEPS

DO AHEAD : Copy the certificate on p. 43 for each student, and fill out the information.

1. Distribute the certificates at the end of the school year.

Tip! ....

If you have a Wild Word party, distribute the certificates during the celebration.

WiLD WoRDs!

This is to certify that

_____

has successfully demonstrated a colossal vocabulary

during the _____ school year.

_____
Teacher

_____
Date

Additional Vocabulary Activities

Create an Eponym

In this independent activity, students create eponyms made from their names, write stories explaining how their eponyms were developed, and design illustrations to accompany their stories.

MATERIALS

• One copy of the Create an Eponym worksheet on p. 47 for each student

STEPS

1. Introduce the word *eponym* (a word that comes from a person's name) as a Wild Word. Share examples of common eponyms.

Examples:

Sandwich was named after the Earl of Sandwich. He loved to play cards for hours at a time, so he had his meat wrapped in bread, enabling him to eat and play cards without getting his fingers dirty.

Stetson was named for John Stetson. He owned a hat factory in Philadelphia that featured western–style hats.

2. Distribute copies of p. 47. Tell students that they are going to "invent" something that will be named after them. Brainstorm category ideas as a group, and list them on the chalkboard.

Examples: food, clothing, holidays, places, machines/inventions, products, music, sports, hairstyles, transportation, games

3. Provide students with time to complete the worksheet.

4. Have students share their eponyms with the class.

OPTIONAL: Display student work on a bulletin board titled "Notable Names."

BOOK BREAK

Guppies in Tuxedos: Funny Eponyms
by Marvin Terban (Houghton Mifflin, 1988)

Introduce your students to eponyms with this fascinating collection of familiar words, including Braille, Washington, scrooge, and graham cracker.

Create an Eponym ✳ ★ ✳ ★ ✳

Directions: Create an eponym that is made from your name. Write a story to explain how your eponym was developed. Include an illustration to accompany your writing.

EPONYM _____

STORY _____

_____

_____

_____

_____

_____

_____

_____

_____

Slang Interview

In this homework activity, students interview an adult to learn about the use of slang from another generation and share the results with the class.

MATERIALS

• One copy of the Slang Interview worksheet on p. 49 for each student

STEPS

1. Lead a discussion about slang. Explain that these informal words or phrases are used in everyday talk but are not generally used in formal speech or writing. Review the fact that slang is usually only popular for a short time. Have students share current slang and discuss why people use slang.

Tip! Remind students to "keep it clean."

2. Distribute copies of p. 49. Assign students the task of interviewing a parent or other adult to learn about words or expressions that were popular when the adult was a child. Have students add their own interview question for item six on the worksheet.

Tip! Brainstorm question ideas as a class first.

3. After students complete their interviews, have them share their findings with the class.

EXTENSION: Have students create a T-shirt design using a word or expression learned from the interview. Lead a discussion about the use of detail, color, lettering, and layout in T-shirt designs. Encourage students to be creative. After students make rough drafts of their T-shirt designs, have them complete their final projects using copies of p. 50.

OPTIONAL: Display the T-shirt designs on a bulletin board or a clothesline using clothespins. Title the display "Stylish Slang."

Slang Interview ✳ ★ ✳ ★ ✳

Directions: Interview a parent or other adult to learn words and expressions that were popular when he or she was a child. Complete this worksheet and bring it to school by _____.

Name of the Person I Interviewed _____

1. What words and expressions were popular when you were a child?

_____ meant _____

_____ meant _____

_____ meant _____

2. What was your favorite word or expression?

_____

Why was it your favorite?

_____

_____

3. Are these words and expressions still used today?

_____

4. What words and expressions did your parents use?

_____

_____

5. How do you feel about the slang young people use today?

_____

_____

6. My Question

_____

_____

_____

15 Minutes a Day to a Colossal Vocabulary • Scholastic Teaching Resources

Uncommonly Good Words Game

In this whole-group game, small teams of students brainstorm more-descriptive vocabulary for commonly used words. Points are awarded for the number of team ideas and the uniqueness of three ideas.

MATERIALS

- Overhead or copies of the Uncommonly Good Words Game Directions and Rules worksheet on p. 52
- Overhead projector

STEPS

1. Lead a discussion about how good writers choose their words carefully in order to communicate a specific idea or mood. As an example, ask students to think of other ways to say *big*. List ideas on the board. Review examples with students, and discuss how each one communicates a slightly different message.

   Examples:

   large, gigantic, huge, enormous, colossal, immense, massive

> **Tip!**
> Write the words on chart paper and post the list in the room.

2. Review game directions and rules on p. 52.
3. Divide the class into teams of four to six. Have each team designate a student to record the team's ideas. Provide each team recorder with writing materials.
4. Have teams brainstorm other words for the word *said*. Provide students with five minutes of work time.
5. After five minutes, have the recorder count the number of ideas the team generated. Teams score one point for each word. Record the team points on the board.
6. Have teams review the words they brainstormed and circle three words they think no other team wrote down. (No other words may be added to the lists at this point.)
7. Call on one team to share their first circled word. Ask if any other team recorded the same word (the word does not have to be circled), and verify. If another team had the same word, no points will be awarded. If their word is unique, award ten additional points to that team's total on the board. Call on the remaining teams to share their first circled word. Continue with the second and third words in the same way.
8. Total team scores, and announce the winning team.
9. Collect students' lists of words, and use them to make a chart of more precise words for *said*. Post the chart in the room for students to use as a writing reference.
10. Repeat this game another time using other words, such as *good, bad, happy, sad, small*, and *win*. Compile the lists and post them in the classroom.

Uncommonly Good Words Game
Directions and Rules

1. The teacher gives a commonly used word to the class.

2. Teams have five minutes to brainstorm more descriptive words for the commonly used word.

3. The team recorder writes down all of the team's words.

4. At the end of five minutes, the recorder calculates how many words they recorded. One point is awarded for each idea. This score is posted on the board.

5. Teams circle the three words they think no other team wrote down.

6. The teacher asks each team to share the three circled words, one at a time. Ten points are given for each unique word. The teacher verifies if another team has the same word. Points for unique words are added to the team scores.

7. The team with the highest score wins the game.

Overexposed Words

In this partner or small-group activity, students nominate words to "banish" from the classroom, present their cases to the class, vote on the nominated words, and create a class list of banished words.

MATERIALS

* Copy of the Lake Superior State University list of "Words Banished From the Queen's English for Mis–Use, Over–Use and General Uselessness." The list is available online: http://www.lssu.edu/banished

STEPS

1. Explain to students that every New Year's Day since 1976, Lake Superior State University has released a list of "Words Banished From the Queen's English for Mis–Use, Over–Use and General Uselessness." If possible, include some examples from the list and discuss why they were included.

2. Have students work in pairs or small groups to nominate words or phrases to "banish" from your classroom. These should be words or phrases that are misused or overused in *your* classroom.

3. Have students present their cases for banishment to the class. Have the whole class vote on which ones to include on your class list.

VARIATION: Have students submit their nominations for banished words or phrases to Lake Superior State University. A nominating form is available on the Web site.

Noah Webster Mini-Book

In this independent activity, students research Noah Webster's life and complete the Noah Webster Mini-Book.

MATERIALS

- One copy of the Noah Webster Mini-Book on pp. 55–58 for each student
- Research materials
- Stapler
- Scissors
- Crayons or colored pencils

STEPS

DO AHEAD: Make double-sided copies of pp. 55–56 and 57–58. Put the pages in order, and staple the mini-books along the spine.

1. Distribute the mini-books.

2. Have students use research materials to complete their mini-books.

3. Have students share their completed mini-books in small groups.

EXTENSION: Have students write and illustrate picture books about Noah Webster's life and share them with younger students.

Tip! ....
Use this activity to culminate a unit on dictionary skills or to celebrate Noah Webster's birthday on October 16.

FIVE QUESTIONS I'D LIKE
TO ASK NOAH WEBSTER

(8)

1. _____

2. _____

3. _____

4. _____

5. _____

15 Minutes a Day to a Colossal Vocabulary • Scholastic Teaching Resources

---

Name _____

NOAH
WEBSTER
MINI-BOOK

When first published in 1828, Noah Webster's *An American Dictionary of the English Language* cost $20.00. That was a lot of money at the time. Design an 1828 advertisement convincing people to buy Noah Webster's dictionary.

Use research materials to help you answer the following questions.

1. When and where was Noah Webster born?

   _____

2. Describe Noah Webster's schooling.

   _____

3. Why did Noah Webster write *An American Dictionary of the English Language?*

   _____

4. How long did it take him to write it?

   _____

5. How many words did it contain?

   _____

6. Describe two challenges Noah Webster faced as he was writing his dictionary.

   _____

7. How old was Noah Webster when he finished it?

   _____

8. If you devoted your life to a special project, what would it be?

   _____

9. Why? _____

Do you consider Noah Webster to be an American hero?

Explain why or why not. _____

_____

_____

_____

_____

_____

_____

_____

_____

_____

_____

_____

_____

⑥

Draw a picture to illustrate what life was like during the time of Noah Webster. Include in your picture three ways life then was similar to life today and three ways it was different.

③

Name three adjectives describing Noah Webster, and explain why you chose each one.

Adjective	Explanation
1.	
2.	
3.	

⑤

FIVE INTERESTING FACTS ABOUT NOAH WEBSTER

1.

2.

3.

4.

5.

④

Wearable Words

In this homework/whole-group activity, students "wear" words to school and teach them to the class.

MATERIALS

- One copy of the Wearable Words Directions worksheet on p. 60 for each student
- One copy of the Wearable Words Homework worksheet on p. 61 for each student
- Paper
- Crayons or colored pencils
- **OPTIONAL:** Camera

STEPS

1. Distribute copies of pp. 60–61, and review the steps.

2. On the day of the event, have students wear their costumes and teach their words to the class. Have students draw self-portraits or illustrate each other in costume.

OPTIONAL: Photograph each student in costume. Display the photographs in the classroom.

3. Display students' illustrations, and bind them into a class dictionary.

Tip!

If students don't have access to dictionaries at home, provide them with class time to select their words.

recluse

noncommittal

BOOK BREAK

Miss Alaineus: A Vocabulary Disaster
by Debra Frasier (Harcourt, 2000)

In this entertaining picture book, a fifth grader named Sage misunderstands one of her weekly vocabulary words and is humiliated in front of her classmates. With a bit of creativity and humor, Sage transforms her vocabulary disaster into a personal triumph during the school vocabulary parade.

Name _____

Wearable Words Directions

On _____, you will "wear" a word to school and teach it to the class. Follow the directions below to get ready for our vocabulary extravaganza!

DIRECTIONS

1. Look through a dictionary to find words that are new to you. List the ten most interesting words you find.

2. Select one word from your list that you like best. This will be the word you will teach the class. (Be sure it's a word you think your classmates don't know!) Record the word and its definition on the homework sheet.

3. Check with an adult to be sure that you understand the word's meaning and that the word is appropriate for our class activity. Have the adult sign your homework sheet.

4. Think of a simple costume to wear as a way to teach the class your word. Do not buy anything special for your costume. Be creative, and use what you have at home.

5. Practice your presentation in front of an adult, and ask for comments. Have the adult sign your homework sheet.

6. Bring your completed homework sheet and your costume to school on the designated date. Be ready to teach the class your new word!

15 Minutes a Day to a Colossal Vocabulary • Scholastic Teaching Resources

Name _____

Wearable Words Homework

1. List ten interesting words you found in the dictionary.

_____
_____
_____
_____

2. Which word did you select to wear to school and teach to the class? _____

Explain your choice. _____

_____

3. Share your word with an adult, and have the adult sign here to show that you
understand the word's meaning and the word is appropriate for our class activity.

Adult Signature _____

4. Fill in the information about your word below.

Word _____

Part of Speech _____

Definition _____

_____

5. Describe the costume you will wear to show the meaning of your word.

_____
_____
_____

6. Explain how you will teach the class the meaning of your word.

_____
_____
_____

7. After you practice your presentation in front of an adult, have the adult sign here.

Adult Signature _____

15 Minutes a Day to a Colossal Vocabulary • Scholastic Teaching Resources

Dictionary Puzzlers

In this independent or partner activity, test students' dictionary skills with Dictionary Puzzlers. Dictionary Puzzlers are interesting questions requiring a dictionary.

MATERIALS

• One copy of the Dictionary Puzzlers worksheet on p. 63 for each student or pair of students
• One dictionary for each student or pair of students

STEPS

DO AHEAD : Review the questions on the Dictionary Puzzlers worksheet to make sure that the highlighted words are included in your student dictionaries. If a word is not included or you already used the word as a Wild Word, eliminate the question and replace it with one of your own.

1. Post sample Dictionary Puzzlers on the board, and have students answer them.

   Examples:

   Would you like to be a **centenarian**? Tell why or why not.

   What advice would you give a **neophyte** swimmer?

   What would you wear in **inclement** weather?

2. Distribute copies of p. 63, and read it over with students. Have students work independently or in pairs to complete the worksheet.

VARIATION: Post one Dictionary Puzzler each day, and have students answer it when they have a few extra minutes. Have students write their names and answers on slips of paper and put them in a box designated for the activity. Announce the Dictionary Puzzler answer at the end of the day. Reward students with the correct answer by putting their names in a drawing for a bookmark, pencil, or other small reward. Have more advanced students write Dictionary Puzzlers for classmates to answer.

Dictionary Puzzlers

Directions: Use a dictionary to help you answer the following questions.

1. Is *azure* a common or an unusual hair color? _____

Explain why. _____

2. Name a *crustacean* you might find on a menu. _____

3. How would you feel if your best friend made a *derogatory* comment about you?

_____

Explain why. _____

4. Name one of your teacher's *colleagues*. _____

5. If someone calls you *magnanimous*, is it a compliment or an insult?

_____

Explain why. _____

6. Does a *superficial* wound require stitches? _____

Tell why or why not. _____

7. Name two things you can do to keep your bedroom *immaculate*.

_____

8. If you think a movie is *mediocre*, would you be likely to watch it again?

_____

Explain why or why not.

_____

9. If you wanted to be *conspicuous*, what would you wear?

_____

10. Name a *picturesque* place in your state. _____

11. Who provides people with *sustenance*, a barber or a chef? _____

12. Name two things your parents might do if you were *febrile*.

_____

13. What would be a good present for a *bibliophile*?

_____

14. What do you think is a fair punishment for *insolent* behavior?

_____

15. What is the *penultimate* day of this month?

_____

Invent-a-Word Mini-Dictionaries

In this independent activity, students make up five words that aren't in the dictionary but should be, and create their own mini-dictionaries. They will include parts of speech, definitions, sentences using the words, and illustrations.

MATERIALS

- One copy of the Invent–a–Word Dictionary worksheet on p. 65 and two copies of p. 66 for each student
- Scissors
- Stapler
- Crayons or colored pencils

Tip!

This is a great time to talk about how new words are added to the dictionary.

STEPS

1. Ask students if they know any words that aren't in the dictionary but should be. List ideas on the board.

2. Distribute one copy of p. 65 and two copies of p. 66 to each student. Have them cut the pages apart along the solid line and staple them together to make a mini-dictionary. Explain to students that they are going to invent five words and enter them into their mini-dictionaries. Remind them to include parts of speech, definitions, and sentences using the words.

3. Have students do the writing and illustrating first and then assemble their books. Provide students with work time at school, or assign the project as homework.

4. Divide students into groups of three, and have them read aloud their mini-dictionaries.

VARIATION: CREATE AN INVENT-A-WORD CLASS BOOK

Have each student invent one word to include in a class book, using copies of p. 67. Have a student design a cover for the book and bind it.

BOOK BREAK

Frindle by Andrew Clements (Simon & Schuster, 1996) Fifth–grader Nick Allen invents the word *frindle* (for the word *pen*) and gets his friends to use it. Soon the word spreads throughout his school and town, and Nick becomes a celebrity. Nick's teacher tries to stop everyone from using *frindle*, but the situation has spun out of control. Ten years later, Nick learns that *frindle* has been added to the dictionary and that his teacher had been on his side all along.

MY INVENT-A-WORD DICTIONARY

Written and illustrated by

_____

Invent–a–Word _____

Part of Speech _____

Definition _____

_____

Sentence _____

_____

15 Minutes a Day to a Colossal Vocabulary • Scholastic Teaching Resources

Invent–a–Word _____

Part of Speech _____

Definition _____

_____

Sentence _____

_____

Invent–a–Word _____

Part of Speech _____

Definition _____

_____

Sentence _____

_____

15 Minutes a Day to a Colossal Vocabulary • Scholastic Teaching Resources

Invent-a-Word ✳ ✳ ✳ ✳

Directions: Invent a word that isn't in the dictionary—but should be! Fill out the bottom of this worksheet. Create an illustration to show the meaning of your new word.

Invent-a-Word _____

Part of Speech _____

Definition _____

_____

Sentence _____

_____

Guess-the-Definition Game

In this whole–group game, students try to guess the correct definition of a word from a selection of definitions invented by their classmates and the dictionary definition of the word.

MATERIALS

• One slip of paper for each student and one for the teacher
• Dictionary for teacher reference
• Container

STEPS

DO AHEAD: Select a word from the dictionary that you think will be unfamiliar to your students. Write the word and its definition on a slip of paper.

Examples: trapezium, convalescent, monger

1. Tell students that they will to try to fool their classmates by writing a believable definition for a new word, and then they will try to guess the actual definition of the word.

2. Write the word and the part of speech on the board.

3. Have students write their made–up definitions on slips of paper and put them into a container. Add the actual definition to the container.

4. Tell students that you are going to read aloud all of the definitions, and then they will vote for the one definition they believe is correct.

5. Read aloud the definitions, including the actual one, numbering them on the slips of paper as you go. Identify the definitions by number, not student name. If a student submitted the correct definition, set it aside for later.

6. Read the definitions again, in numerical order, and have students vote for the definition they believe is correct. Record the votes on the individual slips of paper.

7. Read aloud the correct definition of the word, and discuss it with students. Acknowledge students who submitted the correct definition, and if a student's made–up definition received the most votes, recognize him or her with a round of applause or a reward of your choice.

Tip!
It's fine if a few of the students think they know the definition of the word ahead of time.

Tip!
Encourage students to take notes as you read aloud each definition.

Vivid Vocabulary

In this partner activity, students develop lists of color words to use in their own writing.

MATERIALS

- One copy of the Vivid Vocabulary worksheet on p. 70 for each student
- **OPTIONAL:** One thesaurus for each pair of students

STEPS

1. Have students brainstorm the names of colors they often use in speaking and writing, and list them on the board. Choose one common color word, and ask students if they can think of other words naming that color. List their ideas on the board.

Example: **Red**
scarlet
crimson
cranberry
cherry

2. Ask students which words they think are more interesting and precise, and have them explain their thinking. Distribute copies of p. 70, and have students work in pairs to make a list of interesting color words to include in their writing.

> **Tip!**
> This is a great opportunity for students to use the thesaurus.

3. Have students keep the list in their writing folders for future reference.

EXTENSION: Have students work in pairs to define a list of ten unusual color words.

> *Examples:* celadon, auburn, puce, chartreuse, vermilion, mauve, indigo, teal, fuchsia, azure, saffron, sepia

Provide students with watercolors, and have them mix the colors they researched. Then have students create "masterpieces" using the new colors.

OPTIONAL: Display their paintings, and title the display "A Kaleidoscope of Colors."

> **BOOK BREAK**
>
> **Color** by Ruth Heller
> (Econo–Clad Books, 1999)
>
> In this sophisticated picture book, Ruth Heller combines the science of color with vivid vocabulary to describe the process of color printing.

Vivid Vocabulary ✳ ★ ✳ ★ ✳

Directions: Think of more precise, interesting words to use in place of common color names, and add them to this worksheet. Use this list to help you select color words for your writing.

Red

1 _____
2 _____
3 _____
4 _____

Blue

1 _____
2 _____
3 _____
4 _____

Orange

1 _____
2 _____
3 _____
4 _____

Purple

1 _____
2 _____
3 _____
4 _____

Yellow

1 _____
2 _____
3 _____
4 _____

Black

1 _____
2 _____
3 _____
4 _____

Green

1 _____
2 _____
3 _____
4 _____

White

1 _____
2 _____
3 _____
4 _____

15 Minutes a Day to a Colossal Vocabulary • Scholastic Teaching Resources

Additional Resources and Activities

 The $1.00 Word Riddle Book by Marilyn Burns (Cuisenaire, 1993)
Challenge students to solve riddles using language arts and math skills.
The answer to each riddle requires students to calculate the value of a word
or phrase using A=$.01, B=$.02, etc.
ACTIVITY: Post a riddle from the book once a week as a challenge question. Have
advanced students write their own riddles for classmates to solve.

 Donavan's Word Jar by Monalisa DeGross (Harper Trophy, 1998)
In this short chapter book (appropriate for third-grade students), a young boy
collects interesting words in a jar. Eventually the boy's jar becomes too full,
and he must figure out how to solve his problem.
ACTIVITY: See the Wild Word Jar activity on p. 16.

 Eat Your Words: A Fascinating Look at the Language of Food
by Charlotte Foltz Jones (Delacorte, 2000)
This books is full of fascinating facts about the language of food, including stories
behind food names and expressions and food–related historical trivia.
ACTIVITY: Have students do their own research on the origins of food names and present
their findings to the class. As a culminating activity, have students prepare and bring
in the foods they researched and "eat their words" during a class feast.

 The Pig in the Spigot by Richard Wilbur (Harcourt, 2000)
Did you know that there's a *gnat* in indiGNATion? In Richard Wilbur's delightful poetry
book based on wordplay, students enjoy finding smaller words that are contained inside
larger words. J. Otto Seibold's eye-catching illustrations add to the fun.
ACTIVITY: Have students write and illustrate their own verses using the book as an
example. Bind student work into a class book.

 The Weighty Word Book by Paul Levitt, et al. (Court Wayne Press, 2000)
In this interesting book, an unusual word has been picked for each letter of the
alphabet and is accompanied by a silly story that helps students remember its
definition. Janet Stevens' delightful illustrations highlight the meaning of each word.
ACTIVITY: Have students work in pairs to create silly stories and illustrations that help
others remember the definitions of words. Create a class *Weighty Word Book* with
words from *A* to *Z.*